THE BEATLES G

HAL•LEONARD®
CORPORATION

7777 W. BLUEMOUND RD. P.O. BOX 13819 MILWAUKEE, WI 53213

CONTENTS:

SECTION I—
Melodic Licks That Signature A Song

SECTION II—
Rhythmic Licks That Signature A Song

SECTION III—
Rhythmic And Melodic Licks That Signature A Song

ALPHABETICAL LISTING:

INTRODUCTION

You've all heard of Lennon and McCartney, the songwriting duo, but what about Lennon and Harrison — the guitar duo? Well, that's what you are going to discover in *THE BEATLES* guitar book.

This book is a special work containing a selection of Beatles' tunes arranged exclusively for the guitar. It is designed to provide an accurate look into the lead and rhythm guitar styles of George Harrison and John Lennon.

Although the arrangements in this book are written to embody the essence and style of the guitar works of Lennon and Harrison, the arrangement is not just a transcription of the guitars right off the record. Rather, it uses all of the musical elements: bass, drums, keyboards and guitars, just as the Beatles used them, but all incorporated into one guitar so that you can play the arrangement alone or in a band.

EDITOR'S NOTES

The book is divided into three sections:
1. Melodic Licks That Signature a Song
2. Rhythmic Licks That Signature a Song
3. Rhythmic and Melodic Licks That Signature a Song

SECTION 1

This section includes songs that are most characterized by the use of a melodic signature theme. Songs like *Day Tripper, Ticket To Ride, Julia,* or *Lucy In The Sky With Diamonds.*

This does not mean that you have only the lead or bass guitar in the song, but rather that their importance is the driving force behind the tune. The rhythm guitar compliments the bass and lead licks in this case.

SECTION 2

This section contains songs whose signature is the rhythm guitar. In other words, Lennon's rhythm guitar takes prominence over Harrison's guitar and McCartney's bass or keyboards.

Again, you may have some guitar or bass licks, but they take a back seat to the rhythm guitar.

This section is also important and unique in that it affords a guitar player the chance to learn how to play rhythm guitar patterns which incorporate percussive qualities that any good rhythm guitarist should know. Lennon was a brilliant rhythm guitarist and you'll benefit by learning these tunes as arranged.

SECTION 3

This section contains songs whose signature is both melodic and rhythmic. Let's face it, most songs by the Beatles are a meshing together of melodic and rhythmic elements. Lennon, Harrison, and McCartney did not operate in separate little compartments known as rhythm, lead and bass guitar, but rather merged their functions together. In this section we see how most of their songs are a fine balance between rhythmic and melodic essence. Sometimes it's Lennon's effective rhythm guitar behind the verse and chorus, followed by Harrison blending in a nice solo and bridge that goes back into the strong rhythmic verse section, or Lennon trading off with McCartney's bass or Harrison's smaller lick sections.

It's all put together for you in *THE BEATLES:* guitar book.

In addition, please note that the guitar part is written in guitar tablature to accommodate musicians who read music, as well as those who do not.

For those who do not read, you can follow the tablature numbers, strums, accents, and picking patterns, which you'll learn how to use on the instruction page for tablature (see page 5).

For those who read music, you can follow all of the above, as well as the added musical elements that are included in the tablature line.

All chord changes are shown by the chord frames above the voice line. The voice line gives you the lyrics, melody and which key the song is in.

HOW TO READ TABLATURE

1. TABLATURE is made up of 6 lines, representing the 6 strings of the guitar. The top line represents the first, or highest string on the guitar, while the bottom line represents the sixth, or the lowest string on the guitar. This can be seen in Ex. 1.

2. The numbers on each line indicate which fret, on that particular string, is to be pressed. For example, if the number 5 is on the 3rd line, this means that the 5th fret on the 3rd string is to be pressed. The number 0 means to play the open string.

⊓ = Down Pick or Down Strum.
V = Up Pick or Up Strum.

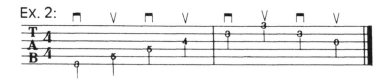

3. A slash (∕) is used to indicate strumming. Stemming and beaming indicate rhythm as in ordinary music notation.

B - Strum bass, or lower strings (the 2 or 3 lower strings).
M - Strum middle strings (the 3 or 4 middle strings).
T - Strum treble, or high strings (the 2 or 3 higher strings).
⁝⁝⁚ (dotted line) - continue previous symbol.

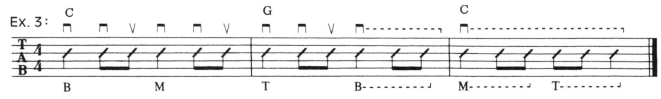

4. (✗) The chordal ✗ indicates a muffled sound to be played on a chord. This is achieved by touching lightly (not pressing) the strings of the chord.

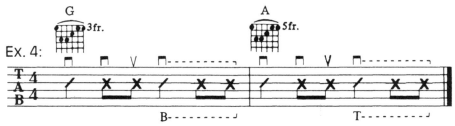

5. (✗) The single note ✗ indicates a muffled sound to be played on a single note. The technique is the same as the chordal ✗ .

6. Common music symbols, such as the following, are also used with TABLATURE.

> = accent
• = staccato
⌢ = fermata

 = Open chord

I Feel Fine

By JOHN LENNON and PAUL McCARTNEY

* Mixolydian mode, not key of C

I'm in love_ with her and I_ feel_ fine._ *(repeat to 2nd lyric)*
I'm in love_ with her and I_ feel_ fine._ *(continue)*
I'm in love_ with her and I_ feel_ fine._ *(continue)*

I'm so glad that she's my lit - tle girl._

She's so glad she's

tell - ing all _ the world _ that her ba - by buys her things,_

7

She's in love— with me and I — feel — fine.—

You Can't Do That

By JOHN LENNON and PAUL McCARTNEY

* Originally recorded in G♭

Day Tripper

By JOHN LENNON and PAUL McCARTNEY

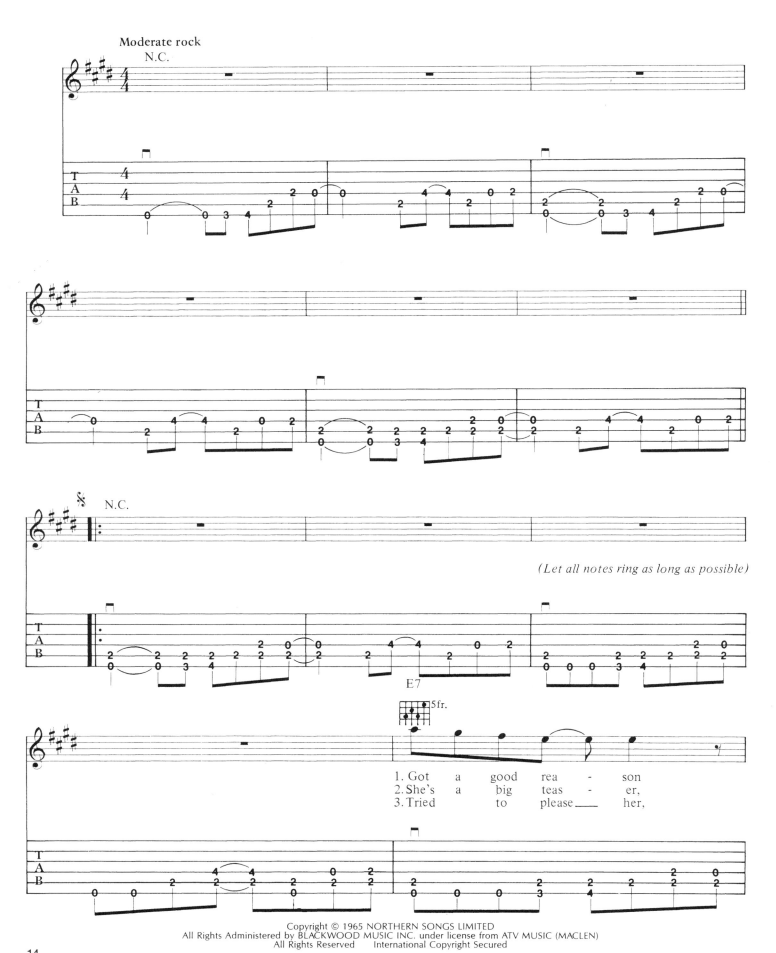

(Let all notes ring as long as possible)

1. Got a good rea - son
2. She's a big teas - er,
3. Tried to please___ her,

Ticket To Ride

By JOHN LENNON and PAUL McCARTNEY

Lady Madonna

By JOHN LENNON and PAUL McCARTNEY

Brightly, with a beat

Use special fingering on "A" chord.

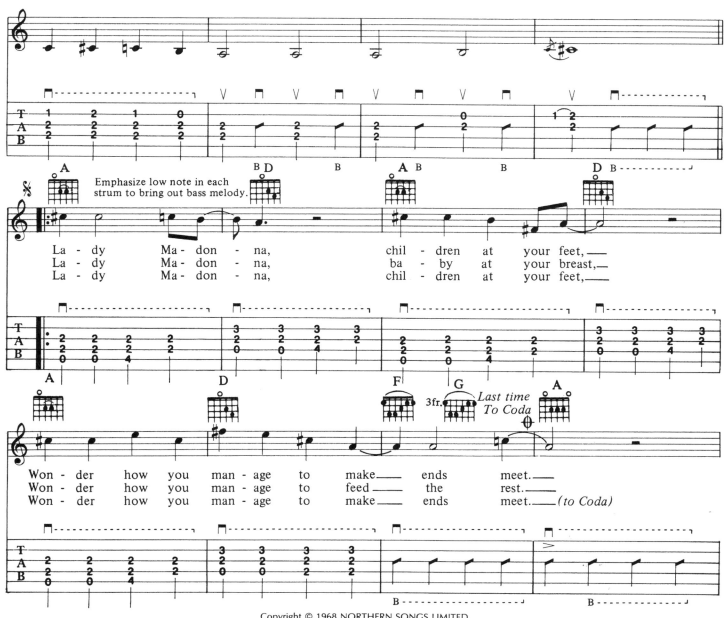

Emphasize low note in each strum to bring out bass melody.

La - dy Ma - don - na,   chil - dren at your feet, ___
La - dy Ma - don - na,   ba - by at your breast, ___
La - dy Ma - don - na,   chil - dren at your feet, ___

Last time
To Coda

Won - der how you man - age to make___ ends meet.___
Won - der how you man - age to feed___ the rest.___
Won - der how you man - age to make___ ends meet.___ (to Coda)

Lucy In The Sky
With Diamonds

By JOHN LENNON and PAUL McCARTNEY

Michelle

By JOHN LENNON and PAUL McCARTNEY

Mi - chelle, ma belle, these are words that go to - geth - er well, my Mi - chelle.—

Mi - chelle, ma belle,
Mi - chelle, ma belle,

sont des mots qui vont tres bien en - semble, tres bien en - semble. I
sont des mots qui vont tres bien en - semble, tres bien en - semble. I

Good Morning Good Morning

By JOHN LENNON and PAUL McCARTNEY

2. After a while you start to smile, now you feel cool.
   Then you decide to take a walk by the old school.
   Nothing has changed, it's still the same,
   I've got nothing to say etc.

3. Somebody needs to know the time, glad that I'm here.
   Watching the skirts, you start to flirt, now you're in gear
   Go to a show, you hope she goes,
   I've got nothing to say etc.

Dear Prudence

By JOHN LENNON and PAUL McCARTNEY

Blackbird

By JOHN LENNON and PAUL McCARTNEY

Slowly

(must be played fingerstyle)

Not to be played off chord positions

Slide up from 3fr. 2nd string

1. Black - bird sing - ing in the dead of night___
2. Black - bird sing - ing in the dead of night___

Take these bro - ken wings___ and learn to fly;___
Take these sunk - en eyes___ and learn to see;___

(lift finger pressure for staccato)

All your life_____ you were on - ly wait - ing for this mo - ment to a -
All your life_____ you were on - ly wait - ing for this mo - ment to be

Black-bird sing-ing in the dead of night____ Take these bro-ken wings and learn to fly;____

All your life_____ You were on-ly wait-ing for this

mo-ment to a-rise, You were on-ly wait-ing for this mo-ment to a-rise.

Come Together

By JOHN LENNON and PAUL McCARTNEY

Moderately slow, with double-time feeling
Tune 6th String to D

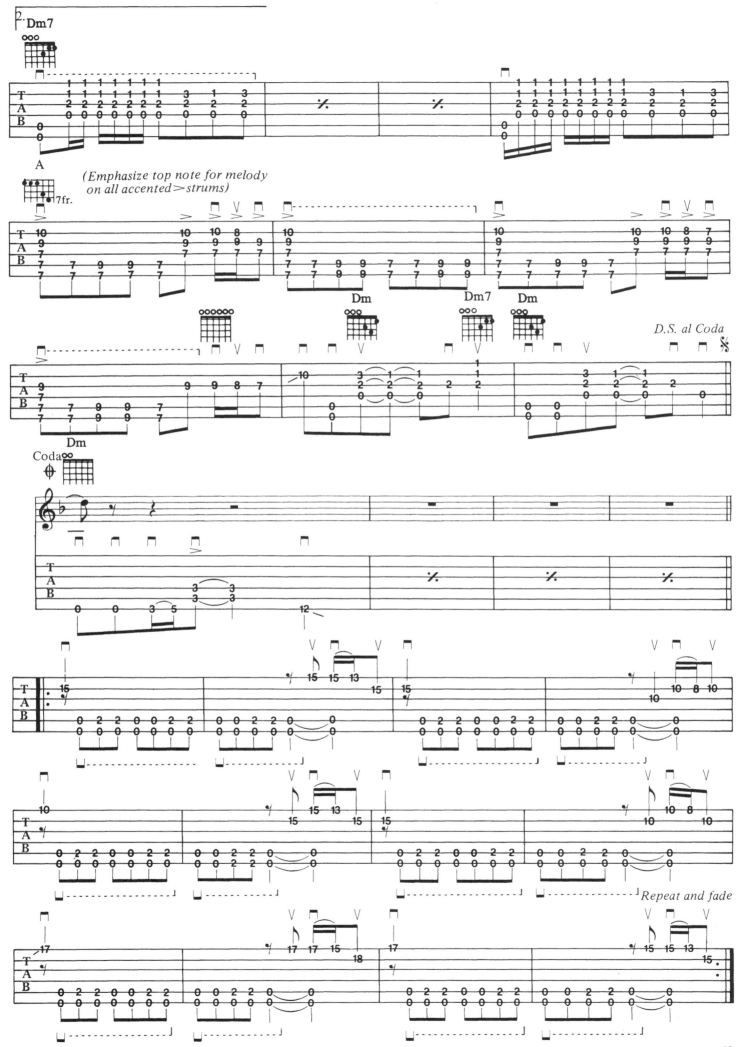

You Never Give Me Your Money

By JOHN LENNON and PAUL McCARTNEY

One sweet dream _____ Pick up the bags and get in the lim - ou - sine._

Soon we'll be a - way_from here,_ step on the gas and wipe_that tear a - way,_

One sweet dream___ came true___ to - day,___

came true___ to - day,___ came true___

to - day.___

One, two, three, four, five, six, sev - en, All good chil - dren go to heav - en.

Repeat and fade

54

Julia

By JOHN LENNON and PAUL McCARTNEY

You Won't See Me

By JOHN LENNON and PAUL McCARTNEY

We Can Work It Out

By JOHN LENNON and PAUL McCARTNEY

Try to see it my way, do I have to keep on talk-ing
Think of what you're say - ing, you can get it wrong and still you

till I can't go on? While you see it your way,
think that it's all right. Think of what I'm say - ing,

run a risk of know - ing that our love may soon be gone.
we can work it out and get it straight, or say good - night.

We can work it out, we can work it out.___

No Reply

By JOHN LENNON and PAUL McCARTNEY

Getting Better

By JOHN LENNON and PAUL McCARTNEY

With A Little Help From My Friends

By JOHN LENNON and PAUL McCARTNEY

Moderato

What would you do___ if I sang___ out of tune___ would you stand
What do I do___ when my love___ is a-way___ (Does it wor-
(Would you be-lieve___ in a love___ at first sight?)___ Yes, I'm cer-

___ up and walk___ out on me?___
ry you to be___ a-lone?)___
tain that it hap-pens all the time.

(Lay side of right palm on strings to get a muffled sound)

You're Going To Lose That Girl

By JOHN LENNON and PAUL McCARTNEY

It Won't Be Long

By JOHN LENNON and PAUL McCARTNEY

Moderately

Hey Jude

By JOHN LENNON and PAUL McCARTNEY

I'm So Tired

By JOHN LENNON and PAUL McCARTNEY

Tell Me Why

By JOHN LENNON and PAUL McCARTNEY

Why Don't We Do It In The Road

By JOHN LENNON and PAUL McCARTNEY

Moderato with a beat

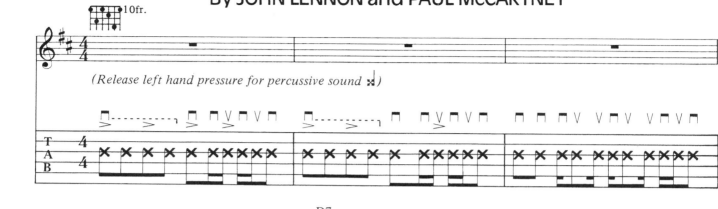

Why don't we do it in the road?_____   Why don't we do it in the road?_

Why don't we do it in the road?_

Why don't we do it in the road?_

Why don't we do it in the road?_

I'm Happy Just To Dance With You

By JOHN LENNON and PAUL McCARTNEY

Baby You're A Rich Man

By JOHN LENNON and PAUL McCARTNEY

Moderately

Rest right hand on strings as you play for a muffled effect for the entire song.
Lift pressure of left hand for percussive sound

1. How does it feel__ to be one of the beau-ti-ful peo-ple?
2. How does it feel__ to be one of the beau-ti-ful peo-ple?
3. How does it feel__ to be one of the beau-ti-ful peo-ple?

Now that you know__ who you are____ what do you want__ to be?
How of-ten have__ you been there,___ of-ten e-nough__ to know__
Tuned to a nat-u-ral E,___ hap-py to be__ that way.__

Lift muffled sound for this one measure

And have you trav-eled ver-y far,____
What did you see__ when you were there___
Now that you've found__ an-oth-er key

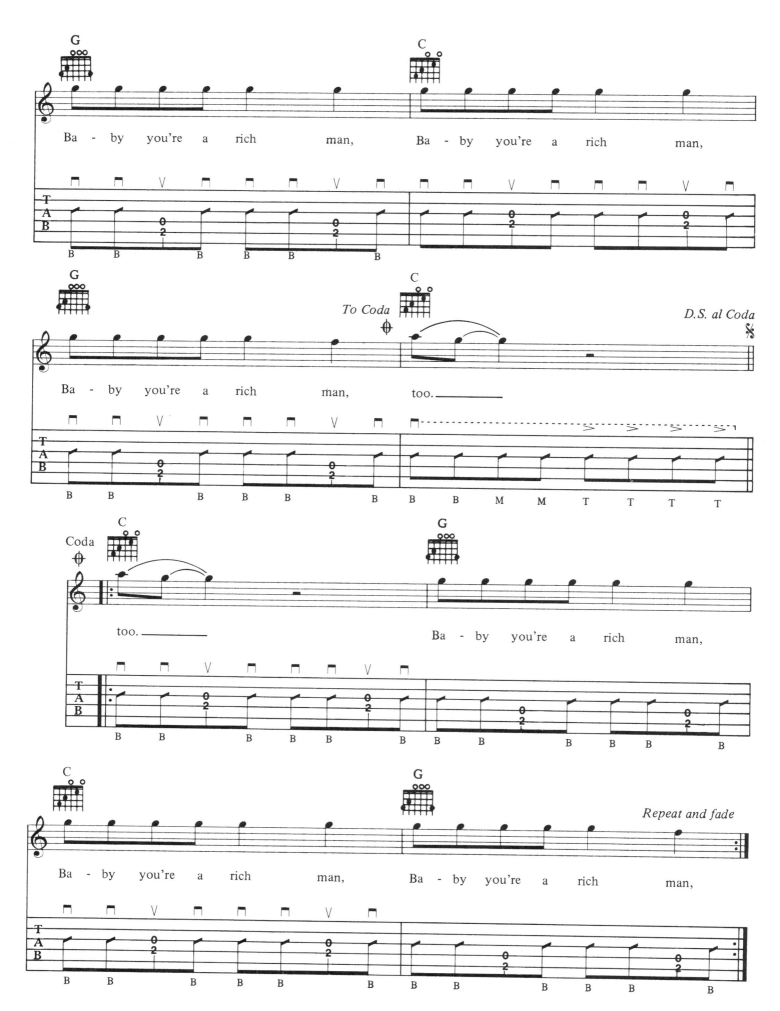

Help!

Moderately in 2   By JOHN LENNON and PAUL McCARTNEY

Back to regular strum

I nev-er need-ed an-y-bod-y's help in an-y way.___
My in-de-pen-dence seems_to van-ish in the haze.___

But now these days are gone,_I'm not so self-as-sured,___
But ev-'ry now and then_ I feel so in-se-cure,___

Now I find I've changed my mind, I've o-pened up the doors.___
I know that I just need you like I've nev-er done be-fore.___

Help me if you can,_I'm feel-ing down,_____ And I do__

110

A Hard Day's Night

By JOHN LENNON and PAUL McCARTNEY

I Should Have Known Better

By JOHN LENNON and PAUL McCARTNEY

3. So wo I should have re-al-ized a lot of things be-fore. If this is love, you got-ta give me more; give me more, hey, hey, hey, give me more.

(Solo)

So__ wo__

You love me,   too.__

119

Eight Days A Week

By JOHN LENNON and PAUL McCARTNEY

Run For Your Life

By JOHN LENNON and PAUL McCARTNEY

1. Well, I'd

1.4. rath - er see you dead___ lit - tle girl, than to
2. know that I'm a wick - ed guy, and I was
3. Let this be a ser - mon; I mean

be with an - oth - er man.___ You'd bet - ter keep your head___
born with a jeal - ous mind.___ And I can't spend my whole___
ev - 'ry - thing I said. ___ Ba - by, I'm de - ter -

girl.

2. Well, you girl
4. I'd

Use 3rd finger on slide.

(Solo)

Little Child

By JOHN LENNON and PAUL McCARTNEY

Oh, yeah, _____ ba-by take a chance with me. _____ Oh, yeah, _____

2. When you're

All My Loving

By JOHN LENNON and PAUL McCARTNEY

Carry That Weight

By JOHN LENNON and PAUL McCARTNEY

I'm A Loser

By JOHN LENNON and PAUL McCARTNEY

some - one who's near___ to me. I'm a los ___

er, and I'm not what I ap - pear___ to be.___

Bring out top note on all accented chords

1. G

2. G

(Fade out on last time)

140

Good Day Sunshine

By JOHN LENNON and PAUL McCARTNEY

Moderate barrel house tempo

* Rock fingers back and forth from left to right for tremolo.

Can't Buy Me Love

By JOHN LENNON and PAUL McCARTNEY

no no no____ no!

Say you don't need no dia - mond rings____ and I'll be sat - is - fied,____

Tell me that you want the kind____ of things____ that mon - ey just can't buy.____

____ I don't care too much for mon - ey,

To Coda

146

mon - ey can't   buy   me   love. _____

She Came In Through The Bathroom Window

By JOHN LENNON and PAUL McCARTNEY

1. She came in through the bath-room win-dow,___
2. And so I quit the p'lice de-part-ment,___

pro-tect-ed by a sil-ver spoon.___
and got my-self a stead-y job.___

But now she sucks her thumb and won-ders___ by the
And though she tried her best to help me,___ she could

Back In The U.S.S.R.

By JOHN LENNON and PAUL McCARTNEY

Moderate Boogie - Rock tempo

153

Anytime At All

By JOHN LENNON and PAUL McCARTNEY

Driving 4

An - y time _____ at all, _____

An - y time at all, _____

An - y time at all, _____ all _____ you got - ta do is

call, _____ and I'll _____ be there *(Emphasize top notes)*

To Coda ⊕

I'm Looking Through You

By JOHN LENNON and PAUL McCARTNEY

Moderato, with a beat

1. I'm look-ing through you, where did you go?
2. Your lips are mov-ing, I can-not hear.

I thought I knew you, what did I know?
Your voice is sooth-ing, but the words are-n't clear.

Hello, Goodbye

By JOHN LENNON and PAUL McCARTNEY

171

She's A Woman

By JOHN LENNON and PAUL McCARTNEY

Fairly bright, with a strong back beat

Release left hand pressure of   sound.

1.3.4. My   love   don't   give   me   pres - ents,
2.   She   don't   give   boys   me   the   eye.____

I   know   that   she's   no   peas - ant.
She   hates   to   see   me   cry. ____

Hold Me Tight

By JOHN LENNON and PAUL McCARTNEY

I Will

By JOHN LENNON and PAUL McCARTNEY

It's Only Love

By JOHN LENNON and PAUL McCARTNEY

1. I get high when I see you go by, My oh my.
2. Is it right that you and I should fight ev-'ry night?

When you sigh, my, my in-side just flies, but-ter-flies.
Just the sight of you makes night-time bright, ver-y bright.

Why am I so shy when I'm be-side_____ you?
Hav-en't I the right to make it up_____ girl?

It's on-ly

Girl

By JOHN LENNON and PAUL McCARTNEY

1. Is there an-y-bod-y going to lis-ten to my sto-ry
2. (When I) think of all the times I tried so hard my to leave her

All a-bout the girl who came to stay? She's the
She will turn to me and start to cry. And she

kind of girl you want so much it makes you sor-ry,
prom-is-es the earth to me and I be-lieve her,

Still you don't re-gret a sin-gle day.
Af-ter all this time I don't know why. } Ah,

Your Mother Should Know

By JOHN LENNON and PAUL McCARTNEY

Fixing A Hole

By JOHN LENNON and PAUL McCARTNEY

Eleanor Rigby

By JOHN LENNON and PAUL McCARTNEY

Moderately, with a steady beat

I'll Cry Instead

By JOHN LENNON and PAUL McCARTNEY

Paperback Writer

By JOHN LENNON and PAUL McCARTNEY

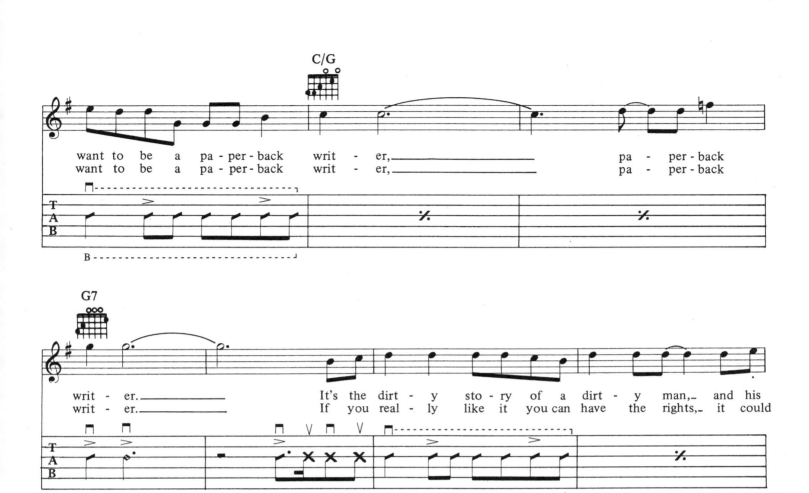

want to be a pa-per-back writ - er,_____ pa - per - back
want to be a pa-per-back writ - er,_____ pa - per - back

writ - er._____ It's the dirt - y sto-ry of a dirt-y man,_ and his
writ - er._____ If you real - ly like it you can have the rights,_ it could

cling - ing wife does-n't un-der-stand. His son is work-ing for the
make a mil-lion for you o-ver-night. If you must re - turn it you can

Dai - ly Mail;_ It's a stead - y job_ but he wants to be a pa-per-back
send it here,_ But I need a break_ and I want to be a pa-per-back

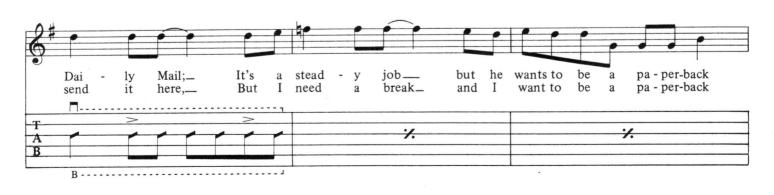

writ - er,_____ pa - per-back writ - er._____
writ - er,_____ pa - per-back writ - er._____

Pa - per - back writ - er,_____

Repeat and fade

Pa - per - back writ - er._____